Original title:
Embracing Change

Copyright © 2024 Swan Charm
All rights reserved.

Author: Kene Elistrand
ISBN HARDBACK: 978-9916-79-233-9
ISBN PAPERBACK: 978-9916-79-234-6
ISBN EBOOK: 978-9916-79-235-3

Divine Revelations Along the Journey

In silent prayer, I seek the light,
Each step I take, a soul's delight.
Through trials faced and shadows cast,
I find the peace, my fears surpassed.

The whispers soft, the guidance clear,
In every heart, He draws us near.
With faith as strength, I walk the way,
Embracing love, come what may.

A gentle breeze, a starry night,
His presence felt, my soul takes flight.
With every tear, a lesson learned,
In fervent hope, my heart has burned.

Mountains high and valleys wide,
In His embrace, I will abide.
For in the storms, His voice I hear,
He calms the seas, dispels the fear.

Through paths unknown, my spirit soars,
In sacred trust, my heart restores.
For every journey leads me home,
In love divine, I am never alone.

The Blessings of the Unforeseen

In shadows cast by doubt, we tread,
Yet grace unfolds where fears dare spread.
The unseen hand guides every prayer,
Through trials faced, love's light we share.

Wisdom whispers in the silent night,
Unraveling truths, revealing insight.
Each stumble a step toward the divine,
In hidden paths, our souls align.

Divine Whispers in the Rhythm of Change

In every heartbeat, a sacred song,
Echoes of faith where we belong.
Nature dances to a timeless tune,
As seasons shift beneath the moon.

Through trembling leaves, the spirit calls,
In changing tides, the heart enthralls.
Embrace the flow, the sacred streams,
For in the change, awaken dreams.

Epiphanies Under the Celestial Veil

Beneath the stars, a longing grows,
In quiet moments, truth bestows.
The night unveils what daylight hides,
In whispers soft, the soul abides.

Each twinkling light, a glimpse of grace,
In unity, we find our place.
Awake! The dawn of knowing near,
In the celestial veil, we persevere.

Seasons of the Soul: A Sacred Shift

Winter's breath brings lessons deep,
In silence, secrets, we often keep.
Spring ignites the heart anew,
With every bloom, our spirits grew.

Summer's warmth, the joy we feel,
In love's embrace, our souls reveal.
Autumn leaves, a graceful fall,
In every season, Heeding the call.

Anointing the Future

In shadows deep, the light will gleam,
Anointing hope, a sacred dream.
With faith as guide, we rise and stand,
Embracing grace, in a loving hand.

Each step we take, a whispered prayer,
In gentle winds, our souls laid bare.
The path ahead, with courage bright,
We trust in love, and walk in light.

The Crossroads of Compassion

At every turn, a choice awaits,
To open hearts, to love's sweet fates.
With arms extended, we bridge the wide,
In every tear, compassion's tide.

In silence shared, a bond is forged,
Together strong, our spirits surged.
In shadows cast, we find the flame,
For every soul, we call their name.

Illuminated Transitions

From dusk to dawn, the journey flows,
With gentle hands, the spirit knows.
In every change, a lesson sweet,
Transcending fear, where hearts can meet.

With every turn, the stars align,
In twilight's glow, our souls entwine.
Each moment clear, like morning's dew,
Revealing paths, both old and new.

A Palette of New Beginnings

With colors bright, the canvas calls,
New journeys bloom where spirit falls.
In strokes of love, our lives unite,
Creating joy, the world ignites.

In every hue, a story sings,
Awakening hope, and cherished things.
Together we paint, with faith in hand,
A masterpiece, divinely planned.

The Breath of Life in Sacred Shifts

In quiet moments, beauty wakes,
The pulse of grace in gentle lakes.
Spirit whispers, soft and clear,
Awakening hope, casting out fear.

With each inhale, life's essence flows,
In sacred shifts, our vision grows.
Guided by faith, we rise and sing,
Embracing the light that love can bring.

Reflections of truth in nature's art,
Harmony echoes within the heart.
Each dawn unfolds a fresh embrace,
In the warmth of God's loving grace.

Through trials faced in fields of strife,
We seek the path, the breath of life.
In sacred trust, we find our way,
As shadows blend with breaking day.

A journey blessed, held by grace,
In every shift, we find our place.
With gratitude, we take our stand,
In the endless touch of God's own hand.

Pilgrimage of the Heart: A Divine Evolution

Upon the road where spirit breathes,
Each step we take the heart believes.
In sacred whispers, love will guide,
A pilgrimage where souls abide.

With mountains high and valleys deep,
Through storms we wander, faith we keep.
Each moment pure, a choice we make,
To walk with light for love's own sake.

Across the lands where shadows dwell,
We find the truth in stories tell.
Each challenge faced, a chance to grow,
In every struggle, grace will flow.

So let us rise with open hands,
As light unites our countless stands.
In every heart, the flame will burn,
A divine evolution to return.

With joy we gather, souls entwined,
The journey precious, heart aligned.
For in this life, we seek to share,
The love divine that's always there.

The Eternal Flow of God's Design

In whispers soft, creation sings,
The rhythm of life that hope brings.
In sacred threads, we find our place,
The eternal flow of boundless grace.

Like rivers wide that gently wind,
Through valleys low, our hearts are twined.
God's design unfolds with every breath,
Connecting life, even in death.

The stars align, the cosmos gleams,
In every soul, the same heart beams.
Within the dark, there's light to find,
An endless love that binds mankind.

With faith as strong as mountain stone,
We journey forward, never alone.
Each moment pure, a sacred gift,
In every heartbeat, love will lift.

So let us dance in life's embrace,
With grateful hearts, we run the race.
For in this flow, we find our sign,
The beauty of God's grand design.

Stars Aligned: The Sacred Path of Change

In twilight's glow, the stars align,
A sacred path, divine, benign.
Through cosmic dance, our spirits soar,
Change beckons softly, evermore.

With every turn, a lesson speaks,
In silence found, the heart now seeks.
We walk with faith, as shadows fade,
In every step, new dreams are made.

The echoes of time, ancient and wise,
Illuminate the depths of skies.
With open minds and loving hearts,
We navigate as the journey starts.

United forces, hope ignites,
Transforming souls, igniting lights.
With each embrace, we find the way,
As stars align to guide our day.

For in this change, our spirits thrive,
In sacred paths, we come alive.
With every dawn, the promise stays,
That love will lead us through the maze.

Faith's Turning Tides

In shadows deep, where doubts reside,
A whisper calls, our hearts abide.
In faith's embrace, we find our way,
The sun will rise to fill the day.

When storms arise, hope stands its ground,
With every prayer, a grace is found.
A steadfast heart, through trials wide,
In faith's sweet touch, the soul will glide.

A river flows with love divine,
Each ripple sings of sacred signs.
With every step, we navigate,
The tides of faith, we celebrate.

As seasons change, so do our fears,
In trust, we wash away our tears.
With open arms, the heart can see,
The wonder of our destiny.

With faithful steps, we journey forth,
Towards the light that claims our worth.
In unity, our spirits rise,
Through faith, we touch the endless skies.

Revelations of the Heart

In silence deep, the heart takes flight,
Awakening dreams in purest light.
With gentle grace, love's story flows,
In every beat, the spirit knows.

The whispers soft, from deep within,
Unravel truths where hope begins.
Through trials faced and wounds that heal,
In love's embrace, our souls reveal.

Each moment shared, a sacred thread,
In every tear, the joy we've bred.
As petals fall, new blooms arise,
In love's embrace, our spirits rise.

With open hearts, we seek the Divine,
Revealing grace, in every sign.
Through struggle's hand, we are refined,
In revelations, peace we find.

The journey clear, the heart ignite,
In every dawn, our hopes take flight.
Through love's embrace, we learn to see,
The sacred truth in you and me.

The Alchemy of Spirit

With every breath, a spark to claim,
Transforming heart, igniting flame.
In sacred dance, the spirit sings,
A timeless song, of hidden things.

The elements swirl, a cosmic blend,
Turning lead to gold, our souls ascend.
Through trials faced, the shadows fade,
In courage found, our fears are laid.

With every step, the magic flows,
In sacred truth, the spirit grows.
As light ignites, our journey starts,
In unity, we heal our hearts.

From pain to peace, the path will wind,
In stillness felt, we learn to find.
The alchemy, of love and grace,
In every soul, a sacred space.

Through storms of life, we rise anew,
In faith's embrace, the light breaks through.
Transforming spirit, we soar on high,
In alchemy, we learn to fly.

Ascension of the Mind

In quiet thought, the spirit wakes,
Untying knots that wisdom makes.
In stillness found, the light expands,
Embracing truths with open hands.

With clarity, the vision shines,
As doubts dissolve, in sacred signs.
In every thought, the love we find,
Ascension blooms within the mind.

From shadows cast, to heights we soar,
Through knowledge gained, we seek for more.
In unity, our thoughts align,
A tapestry of love divine.

As wisdom flows, the spirit grows,
In every choice, the heart bestows.
Ascension leads us on our way,
To elevate, to heal, to pray.

The mind attunes to higher states,
In every breath, divinity waits.
Through love's embrace, our souls ignite,
In ascension's light, we find our flight.

Elysian Growth

In the garden of the divine, we sow,
Seeds of faith that in shadows grow.
With each prayer, the blossoms rise,
Reaching forth to the endless skies.

The sun bestows its gentle grace,
Nurturing all in this holy space.
Roots entwined in sacred earth,
Awakening souls to their true worth.

Through seasons' change, we learn to stand,
In the warmth of love, we take His hand.
With every struggle, we are reborn,
In the light of dawn, no longer worn.

Let the river of wisdom flow,
Carving paths for our hearts to know.
In unity, we walk this path,
Embracing joy, escaping wrath.

And when the harvest comes to bear,
We'll gather bounty in thankful prayer.
Elysian dreams will guide our way,
In the quietude of sacred day.

Ascending to Higher Realms

Climbing the stairs of hope and grace,
Each step taken in a holy space.
With wings of faith, we lift our gaze,
Toward the light of eternal praise.

The clouds may whisper of our fears,
Yet we press on through joy and tears.
With every heartbeat, a promise made,
In the name of love, we shall not fade.

The angels sing, a heavenly choir,
Igniting in us a sacred fire.
Through trials, we rise, our spirits soar,
Unveiling truths forevermore.

As we ascend to realms unseen,
We leave behind what might have been.
In unity with the celestial light,
Transcending shadow, embracing bright.

So onward we climb, with hearts ablaze,
In the arms of grace, we find our ways.
Let our souls dance in this holy ascent,
To the higher realms, our hearts are lent.

The Holy Embrace of Change

In the swelling tides of time, we dive,
Each wave a lesson, a chance to thrive.
With every flux, a chance to grow,
In the holy embrace, we learn to flow.

The winds may howl, the storms may rage,
Yet, in change, we turn a new page.
With open hearts, we ride the tide,
In faith, we trust as we collide.

From shadows cast by fear and doubt,
Emerges light, where love shines out.
With each transition, we shed the past,
In the hands of grace, we're held steadfast.

Embrace the seasons, both harsh and mild,
For in every chapter, we are His child.
Transforming pain to sacred ease,
In the holy dance, we find our peace.

So let the winds of change proclaim,
That every heart can rise aflame.
In the cycle of life, we find our way,
Guided by love, come what may.

Labors of the Heart

In the fields of love, we toil each day,
Planting kindness in sweet array.
With hands of grace, we work the land,
In labors of the heart, we understand.

Each heartbeat drives a noble cause,
In every struggle, we find our laws.
Through trials faced, our souls unite,
In the warmth of hope, we ignite.

The burdens shared, a sacred bond,
In the light of truth, we respond.
With every act of love and care,
We find the joy in being bare.

Embrace the work, the sweat, the tears,
For in these moments, we conquer fears.
Every challenge met with open hands,
In labors of the heart, our spirit stands.

So let us gather in this harvest time,
With grateful hearts, our souls will rhyme.
Through labors of love, we'll find our home,
In the depths of grace, we are never alone.

The Dance of Wings: Finding Ascent in Adversity

In trials we rise, like eagles in flight,
With each storm endured, our spirits take flight.
Through shadows we tread, courage our guide,
In the dance of the wings, our souls abide.

When darkness may loom, and fears grip the heart,
A flicker of hope can ignite a new start.
For in struggle we find the strength to ascend,
Embracing the journey, our spirits transcend.

With faith as our compass, we navigate pain,
In the depths of despair, growth is not vain.
The whispers of heaven, a melody bright,
In the dance of our wings, we soar toward the light.

So let trials arise, let the storms be our call,
For each tempest faced, we shall not fall.
With grace in our hearts, and a song on our lips,
In the dance of the wings, life's purpose equips.

Manna in the Wilderness of Change

In the wilderness vast, where hope seems to fade,
Manna falls softly, a promise displayed.
With each drop of grace, we gather our bread,
In seasons of change, our spirits are fed.

When trials abound like thorns in the ground,
In every sorrow, new joys will be found.
For each change a lesson, in shadows and light,
Manna reminds us, our souls take flight.

Through deserts uncharted, we wander in faith,
Each step a reminder that love never saith,
In the silence of doubt, the heart learns to see,
Manna in the wilderness sets our spirits free.

Let the winds of change blow, let the rivers churn,
In life's sacred journey, there's much to discern.
With open hearts ready, let the promise unfurl,
Manna in the wilderness, a gift to the world.

The Crucible of the Soul: Becoming Whole

In the crucible's heat, where shadows collide,
Our essence is forged, and our truths cannot hide.
With flames of compassion, we're tempered anew,
In the crucible's heart, our spirits break through.

With each trial we face, a treasure reveals,
The strength we have gained, the love that never steals.
Through the testing of fire, our hearts will align,
In the crucible of the soul, we holistically shine.

When burdens grow heavy, and the road becomes long,
In the depths of our struggle, we summon our song.
For in every fracture, a wholeness does bloom,
The crucible holds the promise of room.

With faith as our armor and hope as our thread,
We rise from the ashes, where angels have tread.
In the crucible of life, we merge and we grow,
Becoming the light, in love's gentle glow.

The Sacred Echoes of Transformation

In the stillness of night, where whispers reside,
The echoes of change bring peace as our guide.
Each heartbeat a message, each breath a new start,
In the sacred echoes, we awaken the heart.

From the depths of despair, a new rhythm will sway,
In the dance of the soul, we willingly stay.
For transformation calls, a symphony bright,
In the sacred echoes, we move toward the light.

In gardens of silence, our true self we find,
Shedding old layers, with love intertwined.
These echoes resound, like hymns from above,
A chorus of hope, a testament of love.

So heed these soft whispers, let your spirit sing,
In the sacred echoes, our souls take wing.
With courage embracing, let fears fade away,
In the cycle of life, we transform every day.

Emissaries of Light: Walking New Paths

In the dawn of truth, we rise,
Emissaries of the skies.
With each step, a guiding spark,
Illuminating paths so dark.

Hearts aflame with sacred dreams,
As we follow holy streams.
With courage found in every stride,
We walk where faith and hope abide.

Through valleys deep and mountains high,
Our spirits soar, we cannot lie.
In the whispers of the night,
We find our strength, we share the light.

Each voice a hymn, each hand a prayer,
United, we shatter despair.
With love as the compass, we part,
Walking new paths, open heart.

So let us tread, as kin divine,
In every heart, let love align.
For we are the light, pure and bright,
Emissaries of grace and might.

The Fruits of Transformation in Faith's Garden

In the garden where hope is sown,
Faith blooms brightly, fully grown.
From barren soil, new life appears,
The fruits of love dispel all fears.

Each petal holds a sacred word,
Whispered truths that can be heard.
With tender hands, we tend the land,
Transforming hearts, together we stand.

Trials like storms may often come,
Yet roots grow strong, for we are one.
In the shadows, God's hand we seek,
Nourished by grace, our hearts grow weak.

As branches stretch towards the sun,
In unity, our hearts have spun.
Together, nurturing the seed,
The fruit of faith is all we need.

So let us gather, hand in hand,
In this holy, blessed land.
For in the garden of the soul,
Transformation makes us whole.

Divine Courage Amidst the Winds of Change

When shadows gather, and storms do blow,
Divine courage within us will grow.
With hearts aflame, we face the night,
Guided by faith, our inner light.

In the tempest, we find our peace,
With each gust, our fears release.
United voices raise in prayer,
A chorus strong, dispelling despair.

Through trials faced, our spirits soar,
Holding fast to the heart's core.
Each moment a chance to rise and shine,
Embracing change, with love divine.

With each step, we walk in grace,
Finding strength in every place.
In the winds of change, we stand tall,
Divine courage is our all.

So hold my hand, and let us be,
Shining lights for all to see.
In the storms, we shall not wane,
For in faith, we thrive through pain.

The Holy Light in Darkened Times

In darkened times, when shadows creep,
The holy light, our souls to keep.
With every prayer, we seek its glow,
Guiding us through the depths of woe.

Each flicker of faith a glowing flame,
In unity, we call His name.
With open hearts, we share the load,
Walking together on this road.

Through trials faced, our spirits rise,
With holy light, we touch the skies.
In broken moments, we find our way,
Transforming night into the day.

With hope anew, we banish fear,
The holy light forever near.
In every heart, His promise reigns,
Transforming loss, redeeming pains.

So lift your gaze, believe and see,
In darkest hours, we are set free.
For with the holy light we shine,
In love's embrace, all is divine.

Manifestations of Grace

In quiet whispers, grace appears,
A gentle touch that calms our fears.
Through trials faced, a hand we find,
The sacred love that's intertwined.

Each act of kindness, each prayer said,
A bridge of hope where souls are led.
In darkest nights, a guiding light,
The heart's pure song, a hymn of right.

With every dawn, new blessings arise,
The morning's glow, a sweet surprise.
In nature's dance, the spirit flows,
A testament to love that grows.

Through doubt and pain, our spirits bend,
Yet grace will come, our hearts to mend.
In every moment, the divine we trace,
In every tear, a drop of grace.

Awake, dear soul, to love's embrace,
In every heartbeat, find your place.
For in this life, through all we face,
We journey forth in sweet grace's space.

The Seasons of the Divine

In spring's soft blush, the flowers wake,
Renewed in faith, the earth will shake.
With fragrant blooms, the colors spread,
A promise given, hope is fed.

As summer's sun casts golden rays,
We bask in light, and sing our praise.
In joyous hearts, the warmth runs deep,
The love of God, a treasure we keep.

When autumn paints the leaves in fire,
Let gratitude lift us higher.
In fading light, we find the call,
To harvest peace, to share with all.

With winter's chill, the world stands still,
In quiet grace, we feel the thrill.
The hush of snow, a sacred pause,
The breath of life, the great divine laws.

Through every season, we perceive,
The hand of God, and we believe.
In nature's rhythm, we align,
In awe of every grand design.

Sacred Choreography of Life

In every step, a dance divine,
The rhythms of love, a grand design.
With each sunrise, a chance to sway,
Embrace the light, come what may.

From gentle breezes to wild storms,
Life's sacred dance, it shifts and transforms.
In every challenge, a partner found,
Together we dance on holy ground.

The heartbeat of earth, a drum so clear,
Guides us onward, dispelling fear.
In laughter and tears, the music plays,
We sway in grace, through all our days.

In silent moments, we find our grace,
The sacred twirl, the soft embrace.
As souls unite in the cosmic dance,
We weave our dreams in a timeless trance.

So let us move to the song of life,
Embracing joy and overcoming strife.
With every heartbeat, let love ignite,
In this sacred choreography, take flight.

Hymns of the Unfolding

In quiet hush, the spirit sings,
A melody of love, on gentle wings.
With every breath, a sacred sound,
The hymn of life, where grace abounds.

A journey vast, through time it flows,
Reveal the truths that God bestows.
With every trial, a lesson learned,
In love's embrace, our hearts are burned.

When shadows fall and doubts arise,
Lift up your gaze, to the endless skies.
In unity, our voices soar,
A choir of souls, forevermore.

Through every season, the voice we hear,
Echoes softly, dispelling fear.
In songs of hope, our spirits rise,
We sing our faith, beneath the skies.

In sacred spaces, our joys combine,
In every heartbeat, the divine aligns.
Let us unfold the love we hold,
In hymns of grace, our stories told.

The Pilgrim's Way: Sacred Steps into the New

Each step we take upon this path,
A sacred journey, no aftermath.
Guided by whispers, soft and clear,
We walk in faith, casting out fear.

Under the sky where blessings pour,
We rise with hope, our spirits soar.
The road is long, yet hearts still sing,
In every trial, we find our king.

The stones beneath, they tell a tale,
Of those who walked, who dared to sail.
With open arms, we greet the dawn,
On sacred steps, we carry on.

In quiet moments, we hear the call,
To love and serve, to rise, not fall.
In every burden, grace aligns,
The pilgrim's way, where light still shines.

Embracing change, we seek the light,
In sacred steps, we find our might.
The journey's end, a promise true,
In every heart, the old made new.

A Testament to Flow in Divine Will

In every heartbeat, a whisper flows,
A testament where love bestows.
We stand in wonder, eyes on high,
The guiding hand we can't deny.

Through trials faced, we learn to trust,
In divine will, we rise from dust.
Each path we take, a chance to grow,
In faith we gather, spirits aglow.

Let go the fear, embrace the flow,
In every moment, we learn to know.
The still small voice, it leads us right,
In silent prayer, we find our light.

With open hearts, we journey forth,
A testament to love's true worth.
In harmony, we shall abide,
With gratitude, the soul's true guide.

Together we stand on sacred ground,
In divine will, our joy is found.
With every step, we choose to be,
A testament to harmony.

The Altar of Opportunity: A Holy Offering

Before the altar, we lay our dreams,
In earnest hope, where mercy beams.
Each moment given, we treasure dearly,
An offering true, we present sincerely.

The candles flicker, prayers take flight,
In quiet reverence, we seek the light.
Through trials faced, our hearts ignite,
At the altar of hope, we find our sight.

With open hands, we share our gifts,
In every moment, the spirit lifts.
The sacred space, a promise bold,
Where love and grace forever hold.

As we gather, our voices blend,
In this sanctuary, love transcends.
With faith unyielding, we rise as one,
The altar shines, our journey begun.

Let us remember the power we share,
In holy offering, the love we bear.
Together we stand, united and free,
At the altar of opportunity.

Guiding Lights: The Spirit's Gentle Push

In shadows cast, we seek the way,
Guiding lights shine through the gray.
With each soft breath, the spirit speaks,
In whispered tones, our soul it seeks.

Through winding paths, we find our ground,
In gentle nudges, grace abounds.
With every step, we learn to trust,
In the spirit's push, we rise from dust.

The stars above, they show the truth,
A beacon bright, a guide for youth.
With open eyes, we watch and learn,
In every lesson, our spirits turn.

Through trials faced, we stand as one,
In love's embrace, our journey's spun.
The light within will never fade,
Guiding lights, our hope displayed.

In unity, we walk this road,
With quiet hearts, we share our load.
As we follow, the spirit's push,
We find our peace in every hush.

Whispers of Renewal

In the stillness of the night,
Soft murmurs of hope take flight.
Each heart seeks to mend and heal,
In faith, the spirit seeks to feel.

Morning dawns with golden rays,
Guiding us through misty days.
With every breath, a chance to rise,
Cleansing tears, we touch the skies.

The past is a shadow now,
In prayer, we humbly bow.
With love, we embrace the call,
Together we stand, never to fall.

Nature sings in vibrant hues,
In every leaf, a sacred muse.
Whispers of grace, they intertwine,
Renewed in purpose, our hearts align.

From ashes, new life shall bloom,
In the silence, dispelling gloom.
Trust in the path, the light shall shine,
In whispers of renewal, we are divine.

The Divine Shift

Beneath the stars, we gather near,
In unity, we cast out fear.
A shift in realms, a call to rise,
Awakening dreams beneath the skies.

Every moment, a sacred breath,
In love, we conquer life and death.
The divine spark ignites within,
In harmony, we start again.

Transformation flows like a stream,
Washing away the faded dream.
With open hearts, we share the light,
Casting away the long, dark night.

In silence, wisdom softly speaks,
Guiding the weary, the lost, the meek.
In letting go, we find our place,
In the divine shift, we embrace grace.

Let the rhythm of spirit lead,
In every heart, a gentle seed.
As one, we rise through shadows deep,
The divine shift awakens sleep.

Celestial Transformations

The heavens swirl in vibrant dance,
Each star a whisper, a sacred chance.
In cosmic tides, we're drawn to light,
Celestial transformations taking flight.

The moonlight bathes our weary souls,
In twilight's glow, the spirit scrolls.
With every heartbeat, we transcend,
In harmony, our souls may blend.

Time unfolds like a blooming rose,
In each petal, divinity flows.
The universe speaks in radiant beams,
Shattering silence, igniting dreams.

With open hands, we greet the day,
In gratitude, we bow and pray.
Transcendence weaves through earthly ties,
In celestial transformations, we rise.

In stillness, the cosmos sings,
Of love and all the peace it brings.
As stardust falls, we find our role,
Celestial transformations heal the soul.

Grace in the Unknown

In the shadows, light quietly grows,
In the depths, the spirit flows.
Embracing paths we cannot see,
In grace, we trust, we long to be.

Waves of doubt may crash like storms,
Yet in the heart, a light still warms.
Each step forward, a leap of faith,
In the unknown, we seek our place.

Words unspoken carry weight,
In silence, we contemplate fate.
Through trials, our spirits are sown,
In grace, we find the courage shown.

The journey holds both joy and pain,
In every loss, there's much to gain.
The mystery calls, inviting us near,
In grace, we shed our doubts and fears.

Life's tapestry, woven with care,
Threads of love are everywhere.
In the unknown, we firmly stand,
Grace in the unknown, divinely planned.

New Covenant: The Promise of Renewal

In shadows cast, a promise bright,
A path of grace, a guiding light.
Through trials faced, our hearts refined,
In faith we stand, His love aligned.

With every step, a chance to grow,
His mercy flows like rivers glow.
A covenant sealed, our spirits soar,
In unity, we seek the core.

The past released, we rise anew,
In sacred truths, our vision true.
In humble prayer, our voices blend,
With hope eternal, we ascend.

The promise whispered in the night,
We find our way toward the light.
In every heartbeat, grace adorned,
Together we are transformed.

In love we walk, with open hands,
Embracing all, as He commands.
A journey shared, on holy ground,
In one accord, our peace is found.

Spirit's Journey: From Gloom to Glory

Amidst the darkness, spirits rise,
With whispered prayers that pierce the skies.
Through valleys low, our hopes take flight,
In every shadow, we seek the light.

The sorrow fades, a new dawn breaks,
With every breath, redemption makes.
From whispered doubts to shouts of praise,
In faith we walk through endless days.

From ancient wounds, our hearts now heal,
In whispered love, our truths reveal.
A journey bold, together blessed,
In trials faced, we find our rest.

In sacred trust, the Spirit guides,
With open hearts, our purpose abides.
Through every storm, hope holds us fast,
In unity, our joy is cast.

From gloom to glory, paths unfurl,
In every challenge, love's embrace swirls.
With eyes uplifted, we find our way,
In Spirit's journey, we choose to stay.

Revelations in the Garden of Growth

In whispered leaves, the secrets bloom,
In nature's breath, we find our room.
With every petal, grace appears,
In garden stillness, shed our fears.

The soil rich with lessons learned,
In patient hearts, our hope is burned.
From seeds of faith, new life ignites,
Embracing all, through day and nights.

The sun breaks forth, the shadows flee,
In vibrant hues, we learn to see.
With gentle hands, we tend the soil,
In every act, our spirits toil.

Through seasons change, the garden thrives,
In sacred space, our spirit strives.
With each new dawn, transformation sings,
In nature's cradle, life's joy springs.

In reverence for all that's grown,
In humble heart, His love is sown.
In garden paths, we walk in grace,
Revelations bloom, our sacred space.

Sacred Gifts Entwined in Life's Tapestry

In threads of gold, our stories weave,
In love and loss, we learn to cleave.
Each sacred gift, a voice divine,
In every heart, His light will shine.

Through trials faced, our strength we find,
In every struggle, hearts entwined.
With arms wide open, we share our plight,
In life's embrace, we seek the light.

Each moment precious, woven clear,
In gratitude, we hold Him near.
With laughter shared, and tears that flow,
In sacred bonds, our spirits grow.

In unity found, our lives align,
With every heartbeat, love defines.
Through paths unknown, together we stand,
In life's vast tapestry, hand in hand.

In whispers soft, His love abounds,
In sacred gifts, our peace surrounds.
With every thread, His grace imparts,
In life's tapestry, we're never apart.

The Offering of Surrender

With hands uplifted high, we bow,
To the will divine, we humbly vow.
A heart that aches, yet trusts the way,
In surrender's grace, we find our stay.

In darkest nights, our spirits rise,
The gentle whisper, the holy prize.
Bitterness fades like morning dew,
As peace encompasses all we do.

The burdens laid upon the ground,
In sacred quiet, hope is found.
Each tear a seed, each sigh a prayer,
In yielding, we are met with care.

Let faith enfold like sacred shrouds,
Our doubts dispersed like fleeting clouds.
In trust, we find our spirits soar,
In offering, we seek no more.

In every breath, a hymn of praise,
In surrender's light, our hearts ablaze.
Through yielding, life begins anew,
The offering made, forever true.

Faith's Journey through Uncharted Waters

Upon the waves, our hopes set sail,
With faith as compass, we shall not fail.
The tempest roars, yet hearts remain,
In trust, we find our way through pain.

Every storm, a lesson learned,
In trials fierce, our spirits burned.
Yet in the depths, a calm resides,
Where hope and grace, like anchors, guide.

With courage drawn from sacred wells,
Exploring realms where silence dwells.
The stars above, a map divine,
Each twinkle shows that love will shine.

Together, hand in hand we roam,
Through wilderness, we find our home.
In faith's embrace, we lose the fear,
In every heartbeat, God is near.

The journey starts, with every choice,
In faith's adventure, we rejoice.
Though waters wild may often rise,
Our souls are buoyed by heaven's ties.

Seraphic Visions in the Tempo of Transition

In sacred stillness, visions flow,
Like whispers soft, they gently glow.
Each moment shifts, a dance of grace,
In transition's arms, we find our place.

The shadows fade, revealing light,
As truth unfurls in morning's sight.
With wings of faith, we rise and greet,
The seraphic call, profound and sweet.

Between the worlds, the heart takes flight,
In every trial, we glimpse the light.
The sacred rhythm, tender and true,
Guides every soul toward what is due.

The melody of change we sing,
In every heart, a dream takes wing.
In transitions' grace, we find our peace,
As troubles fade, our joys increase.

Embrace the flow of sacred time,
In every breath, the rise and climb.
For in the midst of all that shifts,
The spirit soars through love's great gifts.

From Chains to Wings: Finding Freedom in Faith

From chains that bind, our spirits break,
In faith's embrace, our souls awake.
The burdens shed, like autumn leaves,
Through freedom's door, the heart believes.

Each whisper of love, a gentle breeze,
With every prayer, the spirit frees.
No longer captive to fear's demand,
In faith we rise, together we stand.

The burdens lift as joy descends,
With every moment, the heart transcends.
From shadows deep, to skies of blue,
In faith's warm light, we start anew.

With wings unfurled, our spirits soar,
Boundless love opens every door.
Through trials faced, we find our strength,
In freedom won, we go the length.

Cherished dreams take flight and gleam,
In faith and hope, we weave a dream.
For from these chains, our hearts take wing,
In love's embrace, we find our spring.

Pilgrimage of the Soul

In shadows deep, the heart shall roam,
To seek the light, to find a home.
With every step, the spirit grows,
On sacred paths, the wisdom flows.

The mountains high, the valleys low,
In nature's arms, the grace we know.
Each breath a prayer, each sigh a plea,
For peace within, for souls to see.

Through trials faced and joys embraced,
In love divine, our fears erased.
The stars above, they guide our way,
In night's embrace, we find our day.

With open hearts, our burdens share,
In unity, we learn to care.
The pilgrimage, an endless quest,
To find the place where love can rest.

In whispered winds, in quiet streams,
The truth of life unfolds in dreams.
With faith as light, we shall ascend,
The journey's end, a loving friend.

A New Dawn's Light

The morning breaks, the shadows flee,
A promise kept, a vow set free.
With every ray, the heart ignites,
Awakens hope, in love's pure sights.

The skies adorned in hues so bright,
A canvas vast, the soul's delight.
In every drop, a tear is shed,
For grace bestowed and faith we spread.

This new dawn brings a chance to mend,
The broken ties, the hearts we tend.
With gentle hands, we weave our dreams,
In unity, our spirit beams.

So rise, dear kin, with open arms,
Embrace the day and all its charms.
In every breath, a sacred hymn,
Rejoice, rejoice, as hopes begin.

With gratitude, our voices raise,
To dance in light, to sing His praise.
In morning's glow, we find our place,
An endless love, a warm embrace.

Seraphic Metamorphosis

In realms above, where angels soar,
Transformation calls from heaven's door.
The broken pieces, stitched anew,
In seraph's hands, the soul breaks through.

A flight of grace, on wings of gold,
The stories whisper, truth unfolds.
In shadows cast, a light shall gleam,
Awakening the sweetest dream.

Through trials faced, the heart takes flight,
In darkest nights, we find the light.
Each moment wrought with love divine,
In every tear, a star shall shine.

In silence deep, we hear the call,
To rise, to shine, to never fall.
A metamorphosis of the soul,
In sacred peace, we become whole.

Embrace the change, let go of fears,
In open hearts, flow love's sweet tears.
The seraph's kiss, a gift bestowed,
In harmony, our spirits flowed.

The Sacred Journey Within

A whisper stirs, a call inside,
To delve beneath where hopes abide.
The sacred journey, steeped in grace,
Awakens dreams we must embrace.

With every step, the truth revealed,
In stillness found, our hearts are healed.
In shadows deep, the light resides,
In silence, love forever guides.

The inner quest, a path so true,
The soul expands, the spirit grew.
With open eyes, we dare to seek,
The voice of love, both soft and meek.

Through ebb and flow, the dance divine,
In let go, we learn to shine.
The sacred within, a holy flame,
In every heart, the same sweet name.

So venture forth, dear kindred souls,
In unity, we make each whole.
The journey's end, a place of peace,
In love and light, our souls release.

The Holy Whisper of What's Next

In silence, a whisper draws near,
The promise of paths yet to steer.
The heart listens closely, calm and bright,
Guided by faith into the light.

Each step unfolds with gentle grace,
A dance with the divine we embrace.
With every choice, a chance to find,
The sacred call that speaks to the mind.

In stillness, we gather our dreams,
Woven together like sunlit beams.
The mystery unfolds at heaven's door,
Revealing what the soul longs for.

Trust the journey, trust the way,
For hope spring's forth with each new day.
The Holy Whisper will not cease,
In every moment, find your peace.

Now open your heart to the unknown,
In faith, let the seeds of love be sown.
For every quest begins with choice,
In the quiet, you'll hear the voice.

Labyrinths of Destiny: Navigating the Unknown

Wanderer in shadows, take a breath,
Follow the path, defy the death.
Within the maze lies sacred truth,
A map drawn in spirit and youth.

Every turn reveals lessons deep,
In the heart, these secrets we keep.
Embrace the whispers of fate's design,
For every twist is a chance to shine.

In darkness, the light starts to gleam,
Emerging from doubt, a radiant dream.
The journey unfolds like a mystic song,
Guiding our steps where we all belong.

Fear not the unknown, embrace it whole,
For in uncertainty lies the soul.
The labyrinths cradle what's meant to be,
Opening doors to our destiny.

With every heartbeat, every sigh,
We dance through the echoes of each why.
For mapped in the stars, a path divine,
The labyrinth teaches, forever we climb.

The Celestial Song of Possibilities

Listen closely to the celestial tune,
A melody rising beneath the moon.
With every note, the heart takes flight,
Exploring the vastness of cosmic light.

The stars shimmer with hopes untold,
Every dream a dreamer holds.
In the harmony of night, we find,
Endless possibilities intertwined.

The universe beckons, vibrant and near,
Each whisper of chance, a treasure dear.
In the symphony of life, we blend,
As seekers of light, we shall transcend.

With open hearts, let's chart the skies,
For in the ether, adventure lies.
The song of creation invites us all,
To rise, to soar, to heed the call.

In unity, we sing the refrain,
The sacred echoes, a blissful gain.
For in every heartbeat, a story we weave,
In the celestial song, we believe.

The Sacred Fire of Reinvention

From ashes, we rise, a phoenix reborn,
The sacred fire ignites at dawn.
With courage, we shed the layers of old,
Embracing a future, vibrant and bold.

In the flames of spirit, we find our might,
Transforming our fears into pure light.
Every flicker, a chance to renew,
As the sacred fire calls us, true.

Let go of the past, let dreams ignite,
For in reinvention lies our right.
With every heartbeat, forge a new way,
In the warmth of hope, we create our stay.

The embers dance with whispers of grace,
Lighting the path to our sacred space.
Together, we rise, a tapestry spun,
In the circle of life, we are one.

So tend to the fire that dwells within,
For therein lies the journey to begin.
With the sacred flame, we shall engage,
Reinventing ourselves, turning the page.

The Gospel of Renewal

In shadows deep, the light shall rise,
With whispered grace, the heart complies.
A burden lifted, souls set free,
In sacred truth, we find our plea.

The dawn unfolds, a brand new day,
With every breath, the old gives way.
In hope restored, we chase the sun,
Through trials faced, the war is won.

Beneath the weight, love's voice calls clear,
From ashes born, our path draws near.
With open arms, the world embraced,
In faith we walk, by love they're chased.

The water flows, refreshing grace,
A river wide, we find our place.
With hands uplifted, hearts ablaze,
We sing our song of endless praise.

In every storm, His peace shall reign,
Through darkest nights, we break the chain.
For in His gaze, we see the way,
Through shattered dreams, we shall not sway.

Cherishing the Unseen

In silence held, the spirit speaks,
A gentle touch, where love it seeks.
Invisible hands, guiding our hearts,
In every breath, the divine imparts.

The stars above, a galaxy vast,
In night's embrace, our shadows cast.
Beyond the veil, the truth does glow,
In whispers soft, His presence flows.

To cherish what our eyes can't see,
Is to find strength in humility.
For in the quiet, His light commands,
A sacred bond, no human understands.

The wind that moves, we cannot trace,
Yet in its dance, we find His grace.
In every heartbeat, every sigh,
The unseen love will never die.

So let us walk with faith as guide,
Embracing all, with hearts open wide.
For in the depths, where silence reigns,
The light within forever gains.

The Spirit's Evolution

From dust we rise, to skies we soar,
The spirit grows, forevermore.
In every trial, a lesson learned,
Through fires of doubt, our souls are turned.

The gentle flow of time unfolds,
With every step, new truth beholds.
In cycles vast, we spin and weave,
In love and light, we learn to believe.

With heart's embrace, compassion blooms,
Illuminate the darkest rooms.
In kindness shared, the spirit thrives,
A harmony where all derives.

Embrace the change, the ebb and flow,
For deep within, our spirits grow.
The dance of life, a sacred song,
In unity, we all belong.

The path ahead, uncertain still,
With faith anew, we bend our will.
In evolution, grace we find,
For all is love, and love is blind.

News from the Divine Garden

In the garden blooms, a truth unfolds,
With every petal, the heart beholds.
A tapestry of colors bright,
Whispers of grace, in day and night.

The fruit of labor, sweet and pure,
Through trials faced, the soul grows sure.
In unity, the seeds we sow,
A harvest full, where blessings flow.

The laughter shared, in playful light,
A glimpse of heaven, pure delight.
In fragrant air, the promise near,
In each embrace, divinity clear.

The roots are strong, in soil of earth,
To nurture dreams, we find our worth.
In every bloom, a story lives,
In every tear, our spirit gives.

So tend the garden, hearts adorned,
In every soul, a love reborn.
With gratitude, we till the ground,
For in this space, God's grace is found.

Radiant Revelations in Shadows of Change

In the stillness of the night,
A whisper breaks the gloom,
Heaven's light begins to shine,
Illuminating paths anew.

Shadows dance with tender grace,
As moments shift and sway,
In every heartbeat, we find faith,
Encouraging us to pray.

The echoes of the past, we hold,
Guide us through the storm,
In revelations sweet and bold,
Transformation takes its form.

With every step, the heart expands,
Embraced by sacred love,
As we walk these hallowed lands,
Connected to the One above.

Heaven whispers, softly calls,
In shadows, we will trust,
For through the trials, the spirit thralls,
Emerging pure and just.

Divine Threads Weaving New Destinies

In the tapestry of time,
Each thread a sacred bond,
Interwoven with pure design,
Crafting destinies so fond.

The loom of life spins slow,
With colors bright and bold,
Every choice, a river's flow,
Stories yet to be told.

Divine hands guide our fate,
As love threads through the seams,
Creating beauty in the wait,
Stitching together dreams.

With gratitude, we take each step,
In faith, we weave our day,
Through every joy and every rep,
The spirit leads the way.

Sacred patterns come alive,
As hearts unite in grace,
In the dance of love, we thrive,
Finding our sacred space.

Ascending with the Spirit's Wind

On the wings of morning light,
We ascend to realms so high,
With every breath, a holy flight,
United with the endless sky.

The spirit's wind calls us near,
A promise in the air,
With open hearts, we shed our fear,
Finding strength in love and care.

Together, we rise in song,
Voices meld in harmony,
In unity, we all belong,
Fulfilling our divinity.

Each moment, a chance to soar,
On the currents of the divine,
With courage, we open every door,
Our journeys intertwine.

So let us dance upon the breeze,
With spirits soaring free,
Embracing all the mysteries,
In the light of eternity.

Sacred Cycles: Life's Holy Dance

In the circle of existence,
We spin with grace divine,
Each season brings persistence,
In life's sacred design.

The sun and moon in rhythm play,
As stars light up the night,
Through joy and sorrow, night and day,
We find our shared delight.

Every heartbeat marks the time,
A pulse of sacred love,
In the dance, we feel the climb,
Our spirits rise above.

With every turn, we are reborn,
In cycles, old and new,
From tender dawn to dusk adorned,
Life's dance calls us true.

So let us twirl with fervent grace,
In thankfulness abide,
Together revel in this space,
In love, we will reside.

The Divine Orchestra's Shift

In the heavens, the symphony stirs,
Angels gather, their whispers heard.
Strings of light played with grace,
As time bows to divine embrace.

Each note echoes, a sacred sound,
Hearts awaken, in circles round.
The rhythms of faith, softly beat,
Binding souls, where hopes converge.

Celestial choirs lift us high,
Melodies woven through the sky.
Together we sing with ardent voice,
In this unity, we rejoice.

In shadows cast, the music flows,
Transforming pains into liquid prose.
Each measure a promise, a timeless gift,
In the harmony, our spirits lift.

As the orchestra plays, we find our home,
In the dance of the stars, we freely roam.
Bound by love, in divine embrace,
The Universe smiles upon our grace.

Insights from the Divine Mirror

Gaze upon the sacred glass,
Reflecting truths that never pass.
In silence deep, the answers bloom,
In spaces filled with spirit's loom.

Each crack reveals a hidden light,
A path unfolds, from dark to bright.
Within these shards, we see our fate,
Where love resides, and souls await.

With every glance, the self we seek,
In whispers soft, the heart shall speak.
Through trials faced, our spirits grow,
In lessons learned, true wisdom flows.

The mirror calls, with gentle hand,
To show us where our hopes do stand.
In the depths of our own eyes,
Rise the dreams that never die.

For in each glimpse, the world is born,
In sacred light, we are reborn.
Through love and grace, we find our way,
In the mirror's truth, we choose to stay.

The Divine Dance of Transformation

In the light of dawn, a circle forms,
Dance of life, through eternal storms.
With every step, the spirit sways,
Transforming night into golden days.

Each turn we take, a lesson learned,
Through ebb and flow, the candle burned.
With grace we weave, the fabric bright,
In the tapestry of love, our plight.

Around the fire, souls intertwine,
In sacred rhythm, hearts align.
Together we rise, releasing fear,
Through every challenge, the path is clear.

In the dance of shadows, truth is found,
As the earth spins, we wear our crowns.
Embrace the shift, let go of strife,
In every moment, we live our life.

For in the movement, spirits soar,
In divine embrace, we seek for more.
With open hearts, we heed the call,
In unity and love, we rise, we fall.

Sacred Journeys in the Winds of Time

In the whispers of the ancient breeze,
Stories linger among the trees.
Each rustling leaf, a tale unfolds,
Of dreams pursued and life retold.

Through valleys deep and mountains high,
We walk this path where spirits fly.
In every step, the sacred guide,
Along the river, where faith abides.

The winds carry prayers, pure and bright,
In every gust, a spark of light.
As time weaves threads from dusk till dawn,
In unity, our souls are drawn.

Each moment lived, a gift divine,
A chance to grow, to love, to shine.
In journeys sacred, hands held tight,
We find our truth in shared delight.

So let us cherish what we hold dear,
In every heartbeat, let love steer.
For in the winds that sweep the land,
We find our purpose, hand in hand.

The Gospel of Growth and Tomorrow

In shadows deep, seeds find their light,
Through trials faced, they reach for height.
Whispers of hope, in softest air,
Bring forth new blooms, dispelling despair.

Each dawn bestowed, a chance to rise,
With every fall, the heart complies.
Paths intertwined, divine embrace,
In every tear, we find His grace.

The journey bends, but never breaks,
With every choice, the Spirit awakes.
Growth, a promise from above,
Rooted in faith, nourished by love.

Awakening to the Holy Unknown

In silence deep, the spirit stirs,
A call to rise, the heart concurs.
Mysteries wrapped in sacred night,
Lead us forth to radiant light.

With open hands, we seek the truth,
In ancient whispers, the voice of youth.
Veils of doubt gently unfold,
Revealing paths yet untold.

Each step we take, guided by grace,
Through darkest woods, we find our place.
In holy realms, our souls will soar,
Embracing the unknown, forevermore.

Celestial Journeys: Shifting Seasons of the Soul

The stars above, a cosmic dance,
In seasons change, we find our chance.
Hearts entwined with heaven's breeze,
Through life's tide, we sail with ease.

Springtime passion, summer's glow,
Autumn's wisdom, winter's flow.
Every season, a sacred song,
In nature's rhythm, we all belong.

From night to dawn, we chase the light,
In every shadow, hints of bright.
Celestial paths weave near and far,
Guided forth by the eternal star.

The Grace of Letting Go

In gentle hands, we hold the past,
Yet time unfolds, and moments pass.
To cherish memories, yet not confine,
In letting go, our hearts align.

The weight we bear, a silent ache,
In surrender's grace, we start to wake.
The river flows, we drift along,
In acceptance, we hear love's song.

Each breath a gift, each moment free,
In trust, we dance with destiny.
Release the chains that bind the soul,
For in letting go, we become whole.

A Soul's Pilgrimage Through the Unknown

In shadows deep, the spirit roams,
Seeking light in distant homes.
The heartbeats echo through the night,
Guided by a fading light.

Each step upon the winding way,
Whispers of truth in soft display.
The stars above, a map of dreams,
Illuminating lost moonbeams.

With every breath, a prayer takes flight,
Through valleys low and mountains bright.
With faith as compass, doubts entwine,
In the unknown, the soul shall shine.

Embracing storms, the spirit sways,
Finding peace in darkened days.
The journey weaves through pain and grace,
A sacred dance in time and space.

So onward flows the endless quest,
To find the truth that brings us rest.
Through trials faced and lessons learned,
The fire of faith forever burned.

The Alchemy of Faith and Fear

In the heart's crucible, both blend,
Faith forging dreams that never end.
Fear, a shadow, lurking near,
Yet hope's light makes the darkness clear.

Through doubts that crash like waves of doubt,
The spirit whispers, 'Hold on, shout!'
Each moment fierce, yet softly held,
In sacred silence, hearts compelled.

The alchemist's touch turns lead to gold,
Transforming hearts that feel so cold.
With every struggle, wisdom grows,
In the dance of light, the spirit glows.

With gentle hands, we mold our fate,
Embracing both love and innate hate.
In the balance, the soul takes flight,
Finding strength in the dark of night.

So let us rise, through fears we soar,
Faith igniting our spirit's core.
Through trials faced, we shall transcend,
In the alchemy, the soul will mend.

Pathways of the Spirit: Renewal's Call

In the morning's gentle embrace,
A whisper calls, a sacred grace.
The pathways twist, with flowers bloom,
Awakening life from silent tomb.

Each step we take, a chance to grow,
In the flow of love, our spirits glow.
Through every branch, the truth will flow,
In nature's arms, our hearts will know.

Renewal's call, a soft refrain,
Through fragile joys and tender pain.
In every moment, seek the light,
For shadows fade when hearts take flight.

With open hands, we gather grace,
Embracing love in every space.
The spirit dances, vibrant, free,
In unity with all that be.

So let us walk this path anew,
With courage fierce, and hearts so true.
For in the journey, we will find,
The grace of life forever kind.

Heavenly Metamorphosis: A Sacred Awakening

From depths of soul, the chrysalis breaks,
In divine light, the spirit wakes.
Through trials faced, the heart ascends,
To meet the dawn where love transcends.

A metamorphosis, pure and bright,
Transforming darkness into light.
The sacred journey intertwines,
Each heartbeat echoes love's designs.

In quiet stillness, truths unfurl,
As stars align in a cosmic whirl.
With wings of faith, we dare to soar,
Transcending fears, we seek the shore.

Awakening in a blissful haze,
We dance through life's eternal maze.
In love's embrace, we find our way,
With every breath, a bright new day.

So let the spirit take its flight,
Through realms of joy and pure delight.
A heavenly call, a sacred vow,
In the metamorphosis, here and now.

Blessings in the Breeze

In the whisper of the trees,
God's love dances with ease.
Every rustle tells a tale,
Of grace beyond the pale.

Through the fields where flowers bloom,
Hope dispels the darkening gloom.
Hands uplifted to the sky,
Hearts are lifted, spirits fly.

Every breeze carries a prayer,
To the heavens, pure and rare.
Promise wrapped in nature's quilt,
In this peace, our fears are stilled.

From the mountains to the seas,
Whispers flow on gentle breeze.
In each sigh, in every glance,
Life's a sacred, holy dance.

Let the blessings rain on down,
In the silence, wear the crown.
With each breath, we find our way,
In the light of love, we stay.

From Mourning to Morning

In darkness, tears may fall,
A heavy heart, the heaviest call.
Yet dawn breaks with a light,
Guiding souls through the night.

In every sorrow, truth will rise,
Like a phoenix in the skies.
Barely breathing, hope still gleams,
Kindled softly in our dreams.

With every shadow that we face,
Faith ignites our inner grace.
In the stillness, hear the sound,
Of promises that know no bound.

Hope's sweet song shall lift the veil,
On a journey where we sail.
From mourning's depths, we shall ascend,
To meet the light that knows no end.

As morning breaks, the world reborn,
Joy emerges from the scorn.
In the warmth of God's embrace,
We find strength, we find our place.

The Heavenly Flux

In the cosmos, stars align,
Divine patterns intertwine.
Cycles flow in sacred time,
Beating hearts in rhythm, chime.

As the rivers rise and fall,
Trust in the Creator's call.
Each wave bears a promise clear,
Of wisdom found in every sphere.

In the storms, His voice will guide,
Through the torrents, He abides.
Faith like a river's course,
Bears us forward, pure and force.

Transformation in each breath,
Life and death, a sacred depth.
From the ashes, beauty born,
In each moment, secrets sworn.

Eternal motion, love unfolds,
In the flux, the truth is told.
With every heartbeat, life's anew,
In the flow, we find our view.

Echoes of the New Covenant

In the silence of ancient lands,
Promises sealed by sacred hands.
A covenant of love proclaimed,
In every heart forever named.

For in shadows, light will gleam,
A tapestry of hope, we dream.
In the breaking of the bread,
Unity where angels tread.

Through the trials, love will shine,
A melody, so pure, divine.
In each echo, hear the plea,
Of grace that sets the captives free.

Hands extended, reaching wide,
In the family of His guide.
Every bond and every vow,
Unified in the sacred now.

In the echoes of the past,
The new covenant shall last.
With each heartbeat, we proclaim,
The love that never knows of shame.

Streams of Serendipity

In the silence, blessings flow,
From the heart where pure winds blow.
Whispers of grace, soft and sweet,
Guide our souls on this sacred street.

In the shadows, light is found,
Every tear a hallowed sound.
Nature's touch, divine and near,
Sows the seeds of faith and cheer.

Gentle rivers, clear their path,
Washing away the burdens' wrath.
Each moment a gift, a sacred chance,
Inviting us into the dance.

Through the trials, joy will rise,
Open hearts, unveil the skies.
Like the streams that never cease,
Filling our hearts with holy peace.

Serendipity, the spirit's thread,
Guiding us where angels tread.
In every smile, a spark shines bright,
Illuminating the darkest night.

Sacred Rebirth

From the ashes, hope shall bloom,
In every heart, dispelling gloom.
With each dawn, a promise new,
Life unfolds in shades of blue.

Tears once shed, now turn to song,
In the symphony where we belong.
Each trial faced, a lesson learned,
Through the fire, our spirits burned.

In autumn's chill, the seeds are sown,
A sacred path, unknown, alone.
Yet spring reveals the vibrant green,
In every moment, God's love seen.

Wounds transform, and souls take flight,
Toward the warmth of endless light.
Embrace the change, the flowing tide,
For in rebirth, our hope abides.

The circle turns, a holy wheel,
In every heartbeat, we must feel.
With each new breath, we rise, we grow,
In sacred rebirth, love's promise glows.

The Light of Transience

In fleeting moments, grace appears,
A gentle touch to calm our fears.
Like morning dew on fragile leaves,
Life's beauty beckons, then it leaves.

Time dances softly, swift and true,
Each second holds a cherished view.
The echoes of laughter, the sighs we wear,
Make us aware of love laid bare.

In twilight's embrace, shadows play,
With every dusk, the dawn gives way.
Savor the now, yet let it go,
For in the present, the spirit grows.

Between the breaths, eternity waits,
In sacred space, love creates.
So hold dear the light as it bends,
In transience, our journey transcends.

Moments cherished in fragile frames,
Spark the soul with radiant flames.
The light we share, so brief, so bright,
Guides us through the longest night.

Chronicles of the Resilient

In the stories whispered low,
Resilience roots where rivers flow.
When winds of change begin to blow,
We rise again, with strength we show.

In valleys deep, through darkest days,
Faith lights a path, our spirits blaze.
Each scar a testament, a tale,
Of battles fought, we will not fail.

With every heartbeat, courage grows,
Through trials faced, the wisdom flows.
In unity, we find our might,
Together shining, hearts ignite.

From ashes rise, like phoenix bright,
Against the odds, we seek the light.
In every struggle, hope remains,
A tapestry woven with joys and pains.

Chronicles penned with love's own hand,
Mapping the journey, a sacred land.
For in resilience, our spirits soar,
United, we are forevermore.

Halos of Hope in the Storm of Transition

In shadows cast by trials, we stand,
Beneath the weight of storms, hand in hand.
With whispered prayers, our souls may soar,
Halos of hope guide us to the shore.

In tempest's roar, we find our light,
A flicker of faith shining so bright.
Through gusts that wail, our spirits rise,
Embracing grace as fear slowly dies.

Each raindrop sings of lessons learned,
The fire of trust within us burned.
With courage born from God's embrace,
We journey forth with steady pace.

As waves crash loud against our hearts,
The peace of love, a balm that imparts.
In every struggle, strength unfolds,
A testament of faith that holds.

With every storm, a gift is found,
Resilience blooms from hallowed ground.
In trials faced, we rise anew,
Halos of hope, a sacred view.

The Holy Embrace of New Beginnings

In the cradle of dawn's gentle grace,
New beginnings find their sacred place.
With every breath, life starts to sing,
In the holy embrace of awakening.

As petals unfurl beneath the sun,
The journey of faith has just begun.
With open hearts, we seek to know,
The blessings that come from above.

In whispers soft, the Spirit calls,
Guiding us gently as fear sometimes falls.
Each moment anew, a chance to grow,
In the promise of love, let our spirits flow.

With trust we step on paths divine,
From shadows past, we lift and shine.
The holy embrace surrounds us tight,
Igniting souls with radiant light.

In sacred rhythms, our hearts will dance,
Embracing the presence of holy chance.
Through trials faced and choices made,
New beginnings blossom, never to fade.

Spirit's Rebirth: Trusting the Divine Path

When night seems long and hope runs thin,
The Spirit whispers, 'Hold fast within.'
For every ending births a new start,
Trusting the Divine with an open heart.

In stillness found, we shed our chains,
The weight of worry, the ache of pains.
With every tear, a blessing flows,
In Spirit's rebirth, our essence glows.

With faith as our guide, we walk the road,
Embracing each step, lightening our load.
For in the shadows, love's light will bloom,
Transforming our fears, dispelling the gloom.

In the dance of life, we trust and sway,
With each breath taken, we find our way.
The Divine path unfolds before our eyes,
Leading us gently toward the skies.

Through valleys deep and mountains high,
With open arms, we learn to fly.
For Spirit's rebirth reveals the truth,
In trusting the Divine, we reclaim our youth.

The Pilgrim's Heart: Paths Untraveled

With pilgrim's heart, we roam the land,
Embracing change, we take our stand.
On paths untraveled, faith ignites,
Guided by stars on lunar nights.

In every step, a story unfolds,
The whispers of wisdom, brave and bold.
With courage anew, we bear the weight,
For every journey leads to fate.

Through valleys rich and mountains grand,
The beauty of life, near at hand.
With open souls, we share our grace,
In unity's warmth, we find our place.

With hearts ablaze, we seek the light,
Transforming shadows, banishing fright.
In the pilgrimage, we come alive,
Finding the strength in love to thrive.

Each road we tread bears sacred worth,
Connecting us deeply to the earth.
Through faith and hope, we rise as one,
In the pilgrim's heart, our work is done.

Revelations in Life's Sacred Canvas

In the quiet of dawn's embrace,
Whispers of truth start to bloom.
Colors of faith paint our path,
Guiding souls through the gloom.

Every stroke of divine grace,
Tells a story, unfolds the dream.
In shadows, we find our place,
Illuminated by love's beam.

Hearts entwined in sacred dance,
Each moment a brush with the light.
In the canvas of circumstance,
We find the strength to ignite.

In the tapestry of the world,
Our spirits intertwine and soar.
With every prayer softly unfurled,
We touch the divine evermore.

Gathered here in life's embrace,
We witness creation's fine art.
A masterpiece of endless grace,
Reflecting love from the heart.

The Light of New Horizons

At dawn, when shadows flee,
Hope rises with the sun.
Every ray a promise sweet,
A new day has begun.

In the valleys of despair,
Faith is our gentle guide.
With each step, we learn to care,
In love, we can confide.

Mountains whisper to the skies,
Our burdens lifted high.
In the light, we find our ties,
As hearts begin to fly.

Through trials, our spirits grow,
Resilience shines like gold.
With gratitude, we come to know,
New horizons must unfold.

Together on this sacred quest,
We journey hand in hand.
In unity, we find our rest,
As part of heaven's plan.

From Ashes to Altars: A Sacred Renewing

From ashes, new life shall arise,
Resilient like the dawn.
Through pain and trials, we realize,
In sorrow, justice is born.

Each altar, a place to reflect,
Moments of beauty from pain.
In the silence, we connect,
Our spirits cleansed by the rain.

With hands raised in surrender,
We release what no longer serves.
In the depth, we find the tender,
Our hearts' pure, sacred curves.

As the soul begins to mend,
In forgiveness, we are free.
From the ashes, we ascend,
Embracing our true decree.

In every crack of the heart,
A light shines ever bright.
From ashes, we create art,
Transforming darkness to light.

Mosaic of Divine Transformations

In the fragments of our past,
We find a sacred song.
Each piece a lesson cast,
Together we grow strong.

From bitterness to sweet grace,
We weave our lives anew.
In each smile, in each embrace,
The divine shines through.

Colors blend in harmony,
Creating a vibrant sphere.
In love's tender symphony,
We overcome our fear.

Every trial a brush's mark,
Each triumph a shining gem.
In the whole, we find the spark,
The essence of our poem.

Together in this sacred dance,
We celebrate life's embrace.
In unity, we seize the chance,
To create with divine grace.

Threads of Divine Design

In the tapestry of grace, we find,
Each thread, a story, intertwined.
Woven by hands unseen above,
Stitched with care, and bound by love.

In every twist, in every turn,
Lessons of faith, in our hearts we learn.
A light that shines in darkest night,
Guiding us forth, into the light.

Through trials faced, and joys embraced,
In the fabric of life, we find our place.
The patterns grand, the threads so fine,
Reveal the beauty of the divine.

With every prayer, a stitch we make,
In the sacred quilt, we rise, awake.
Together, as one, in unity we dwell,
Within the weave of a heavenly spell.

Let us cherish each pure strand,
Crafted by the Almighty's hand.
In this design, eternally we'll thrive,
For through His love, we come alive.

Mosaic of Seasons

In spring's bloom, our spirits sigh,
Awakening dreams, beneath the sky.
The earth rejoices, colors bright,
As flowers dance in morning light.

Summer's warmth, a gentle embrace,
In each heartbeat, we find our place.
With sunlit days and starlit nights,
Our souls are lifted, taking flight.

Autumn whispers tales of change,
A sacred cycle, both sweet and strange.
Leaves like fire, they fall and spin,
Reminding us of the life within.

Winter's hush brings silence deep,
In faith, we trust, in peace we keep.
The stillness calls us to reflect,
On love's presence, we reconnect.

In each season, God's hand we trace,
A mosaic painted with divine grace.
Together we journey on this quest,
In every season, we find our rest.

The Pathway of the Spirit

Along the path, where shadows dwell,
A whisper soft, a sacred spell.
Each step we take, a call to prayer,
In the stillness, God is there.

Through valleys low, and mountains high,
The spirit soars, it cannot die.
With steadfast hearts, we seek the way,
In every moment, come what may.

The journey bends, with twists and turns,
In every trial, the spirit learns.
With faith as guide, we walk with grace,
Hand in hand, we seek His face.

In love's embrace, we find our song,
A melody where we belong.
With open hearts, we share the light,
Together we rise, dispelling night.

So let us tread this path with joy,
Each heart, a vessel, none could destroy.
Through the trials, we stand as one,
On the pathway of the Spirit, we run.

A Symphony of Transformation

In the silence deep, the notes arise,
A symphony for the soul, the skies.
Each heart a drum, each breath a chime,
In harmony, we dance through time.

With every struggle, a new refrain,
Beauty found in joy and pain.
The chords of life, both sharp and sweet,
Guide us to the rhythm of our feet.

A crescendo builds, a love profound,
In every heartbeat, grace is found.
The orchestra plays, a timeless song,
Inviting us to join along.

In moments fleeting, the echoes call,
Transforming shadows, embracing all.
With voices raised, we sing as one,
In unity, our hearts have won.

So let this symphony play on,
With faithful hearts, we carry on.
Through every note, in faith we stand,
A transformation, divine and grand.

Blessings of the Unknown: Faith's Promise

In shadows where we tread, unseen,
Faith whispers hope, a gentle gleam.
Each step into the vast unknown,
A promise held where love is sown.

In trials faced with hearts so meek,
Guiding hands, the strong we seek.
Through storms that rage and winds that howl,
We find our peace, on faith we prowl.

The paths may twist, and fears may rise,
Yet in the depths, a strength surprise.
With every tear, a blessing grows,
In trust, the light of truth bestows.

So let us walk, both brave and bold,
In dreams of silver, stitched with gold.
The unknown calls, a sacred jest,
WIth faith our hearts find perfect rest.

The Call of New Horizons: A Heavenly Invitation

Beneath the sky, where eagles soar,
A whisper stirs, to seek for more.
New horizons beckon, wide and free,
An invitation to the soul's decree.

With each dawn that breaks, a fresh embrace,
The light of heaven, our sacred space.
We journey forth on pathways bright,
With heavenly hosts, our guiding light.

Let faith ignite the flame within,
To follow dreams, where new life's been.
In every moment, grace is found,
A holy echo, a joyful sound.

Together we rise, together we stand,
With hearts aligned, a faithful band.
In every challenge, we shall find,
New horizons, with love entwined.

The Divine Tapestry of Life's Changes

Threads of gold weave through the night,
A tapestry, both dark and bright.
In every change, a pattern spun,
Divine design, the work begun.

Each joy and sorrow, a stitch in time,
Creating beauty, a sacred rhyme.
With every heartbeat, life reveals,
The loving hands that fate conceals.

As seasons shift from young to old,
In every wrinkle, stories told.
Embrace the flow, let worries cease,
In the tapestry, find sweet release.

For in the dance of birth and death,
The sacred rhythm fills our breath.
The divine weaves through all we face,
Gracing our lives with boundless grace.

Manifesting Miracles in Times of Turmoil

In darkest hours, when hope is thin,
A flicker starts, igniting within.
The heart believes and faith takes flight,
Miracles bloom with guiding light.

In the chaos, calm we seek,
With mindful hearts that dare to speak.
For every burden, there's a way,
A miracle born from night to day.

Each tear we shed becomes a seed,
Of strength and love in times of need.
With every prayer, let spirits rise,
A chorus sings beneath the skies.

So hold on tight, embrace the fight,
In every shadow, find the light.
Together we stand, our spirits soar,
Manifesting miracles, forevermore.

The Sacred Script of Destiny's Changes

In shadows cast by time's soft hand,
We search for purpose in this land.
A whisper calls through ancient scrolls,
Unraveling the truth of souls.

Each turn of fate, a lesson learned,
In quiet fires, our spirits burned.
We journey forth, a guided trail,
With faith, we rise, we do not fail.

The storms may rage, the dark may loom,
Yet in our hearts, there's light to bloom.
In every tear, a seed is sown,
The growth of love, a strength we've grown.

Let every moment breathe divine,
In sacred script, our lives align.
As destiny reveals its face,
We walk together in His grace.

So trust the path, though winding, long,
Each step prepares us to be strong.
In every choice, a truth appears,
Embrace the journey, calm your fears.

Transfiguration: A Testament of the Spirit

In silent prayer, the spirit soars,
Transcending pain, it opens doors.
A glimpse of glory, love entwined,
The heart awakens, soul aligned.

Each moment shared, each worshiped hour,
Transfigured life becomes His power.
In shadows deep, find sacred light,
Transform our burdens, make them bright.

With every breath, a hymn ascends,
In unity, our journey bends.
We rise renewed, through trials faced,
In grace embraced, we are interlaced.

The spirit speaks in gentle sighs,
In sacred echoes, wisdom flies.
Together bound, we walk this road,
A testament of love bestowed.

Let faith ignite, let hope abide,
In every heart, the truth resides.
Our destinies, a hand in hand,
In transfiguration, we understand.

The Choir of Change in Sacred Harmony

In gentle whispers, change unfolds,
A choir sings, its power bold.
Each voice a note, a story shared,
In sacred harmony, we're prepared.

As seasons turn, the heart can swell,
In unity forged, we find our well.
The melody of life resounds,
In every pulse, our spirit grounds.

Through trials faced, the songs arise,
In reverence, we lift our eyes.
A symphony of love and grace,
In every note, a warm embrace.

Let every heartbeat join the choir,
With hopes ablaze, our souls aspire.
In change, we find our strength anew,
A sacred bond, forever true.

Together on this path we tread,
With joy and faith, our spirits fed.
In sacred harmony, we sing,
The choir of change, our offering.

Divine Interludes: Embracing Life's Unfolding

In quiet moments, grace descends,
Divine interludes that time transcends.
With every breath, a gift of light,
Embracing life, we take our flight.

The tapestry of time unwinds,
In every thread, a love that binds.
Through laughter shared and sorrows borne,
In all our trials, new paths are worn.

Within the ebb and flow we find,
A sacred rhythm, gently timed.
With open hearts, we greet the dawn,
In every ending, hope is drawn.

Let not the shadows steal our grace,
For in the dark, love finds its place.
The journey's course, we'll gladly tread,
With every step, our spirits fed.

So trust the flow, let courage sing,
In divine embrace, we find our wings.
For life unfolds, a wondrous scroll,
In every interlude, we are whole.

Milton Keynes UK
Ingram Content Group UK Ltd.
UKHW020042271124
451585UK00012B/1003